Breakthrough Inventions

INVENTING THE COMPUTER

Marsha Groves

Crabtree Publishing Company
www.crabtreebooks.com

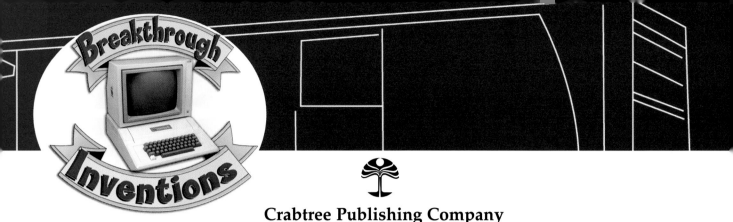

Crabtree Publishing Company

www.crabtreebooks.com

Coordinating editor: Ellen Rodger

Series editor: Adrianna Morganelli

Designer and production coordinator: Rosie Gowsell

Production assistant: Samara Parent

Scanning technician: Arlene Arch-Wilson

Art director: Rob MacGregor

Prepress technician: Nancy Johnson

Project development, editing, photo editing, and layout
First Folio Resource Group, Inc.: Tom Dart, Sarah Gleadow, Debbie Smith

Photo research
Maria DeCambra, Linda Tanaka

Consultants: Dr. E.H. Dooijes, Curator, The Computer Museum, at the University of Amsterdam; Dag Spicer, Senior Curator, Computer History Museum; David Weil, Curator, The San Diego Computer Museum

Photographs: AP Photo/Paul Sakuma/CP: p. 22 (right); Courtesy of Apple: p. 29 (right); Bettmann/Corbis: p. 11 (left), p. 16 (right); Bryan Blackburn: p. 18; Bletchley Park Trust/Science & Society Picture Library: p. 10; Paul Buck/AFP/Getty Images: p. 16 (left); CERN/Science & Society Picture Library: p. 25 (right); Computer History Museum: p. 13 (top), p. 14, p. 24 (right); Jerry Cooke/Corbis: cover (center right); Digital Art/Corbis: p. 31 (left); Dr. Douglas Engelbart and Bootstrap Institute/Alliance: p. 19 (bottom right); Werner Forman/Art Resource, NY: p. 4 (right); Pascal Goetgheluck/Science Photo Library: p. 27 (left); Granger Collection, New York: p. 5

(bottom), p. 7 (bottom), p. 9 (left); IBM Corporate Archives: p. 9 (right), p. 13 (bottom), p. 15 (left), p. 19 (bottom left); istockphoto.com/Darryl Brooks: p. 28 (bottom); istockphoto.com/cb34inc: p. 21 (bottom); istockphoto.com/Scott Dunlap: p. 23 (bottom); istockphoto.com/Sergey Kashkin: p. 17 (right); istockphoto.com/Arthur Kwiatkowski: cover (top right), contents page; istockphoto.com/picpics: p. 30 (right); istockphoto.com/Amanda Rohde: pp. 6–7; istockphoto.com/Ian Smith: p. 21 (top); istockphoto.com/Leah-Anne Thompson: p. 26 (bottom); istockphoto.com/Jaimie D. Travis: p. 28 (top); Ruth Kikin-Gil, innovator and experience designer, Photo: Ivan Gasparini, 2005: p. 30 (left); James King-Holmes/Photo Researchers, Inc.: p. 31 (right); Erich Lessing/Art Resource, NY: p. 7 (top); Los Alamos National Laboratory/Science Photo Library: p. 11 (right); Lumeta Corporation: p. 24 (left); Musée de la Poste, Paris, France/Peter Willi/The Bridgeman Art Library: p. 5 (top); David Parker/Seagate Microelectronics Ltd./Science Photo Library: p. 17 (left); Alfred Pasieka/Photo Researchers, Inc.: p. 15 (right); Reuters/Corbis: p. 23 (top); Royalty-Free/Corbis: p. 29 (left); Science Museum/Science & Society Picture Library: title page (top), copyright page, p. 6 (top), p. 8, p. 12, p. 19 (top); Other images from stock CD.

Cover: A few decades ago, computers were expensive systems that only a few scientists and large businesses used. Today, inexpensive computers are used for work and play in many homes, schools, and businesses.

Title page: The inside of a computer hard drive looks deceptively simple.

Contents page: By moving the mouse and clicking the mouse buttons, computer users give the computer commands.

Library and Archives Canada Cataloguing in Publication

Groves, Marsha
    Inventing the Computer / Marsha Groves.

(Breakthrough Inventions)
Includes index.
ISBN 978-0-7787-2816-0 (bound)
ISBN 978-0-7787-2838-2 (pbk.)

    1. Computers--History--Juvenile literature. 2. Inventions--Juvenile literature. I. Title. II. Series.

QA76.23.G76 2007   j004   C2007-900640-X

Library of Congress Cataloging-in-Publication Data

Groves, Marsha.
    Inventing the Computer / written by Marsha Groves.
      p. cm. -- (Breakthrough Inventions)
    Includes index.
    ISBN-13: 978-0-7787-2816-0 (rlb)
    ISBN-10: 0-7787-2816-1 (rlb)
    ISBN-13: 978-0-7787-2838-2 (pb)
    ISBN-10: 0-7787-2838-2 (pb)
  1. Computers--Juvenile literature. I. Title. II. Series.

QA76.23.G75 2007
004--dc22   2007002919
                       LC

Crabtree Publishing Company

www.crabtreebooks.com   1-800-387-7650

Published in Canada
Crabtree Publishing
616 Welland Ave.
St. Catharines, Ontario
L2M 5V6

Published in the United States
Crabtree Publishing
PMB16A
350 Fifth Ave., Suite 3308
New York, NY 10118

Published in the United Kingdom
Crabtree Publishing
White Cross Mills
High Town, Lancaster
LA1 4XS

Published in Australia
Crabtree Publishing
386 Mt. Alexander Rd.
Ascot Vale (Melbourne)
VIC 3032

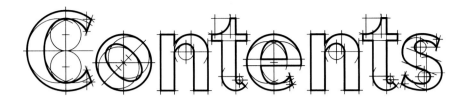Contents

A New Age

L ess than 70 years ago, mathematicians, scientists, and engineers developed the first computers. It is now difficult to imagine a world without these electronic devices. People use computers to calculate, store information, send messages, and control other machines, all with much greater speed and accuracy than humans working alone or using simple mechanical **devices.**

*Incan **officials used clusters of knotted strings, called** quipu**, to keep track of the** **size of llama herds and the** **numbers of crops.***

Remembering the Time before Computers

Before there was writing, and thousands of years before computers were invented, people told stories, recited rhymes, sang songs, and drew pictures to help them remember important dates and events. They cut notches in sticks to record the number of animals they owned, the quantity of grain they harvested, and the amount of money they owed or had loaned. In cultures where writing became important, more and more information was stored in books, scrolls, and other documents.

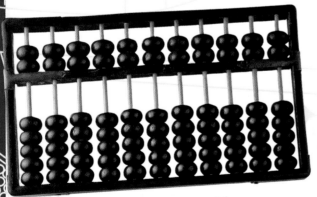

The abacus was originally a table or board divided into sections on which small stones or counters were moved. By 1300 A.D., the style of abacus shown here, with beads that slide on wires, had been developed in China.

Calculating before Computers

Ever since numbers and arithmetic were invented thousands of years ago, people have looked for ways to help them add, subtract, multiply, and divide more quickly and accurately. By 500 B.C., in what is now the country of Iraq, a tool called a counting table, or abacus, was widely used. For 2,000 years in much of Europe, North Africa, and Asia, abacuses were the most common tools to help with calculations. Government officials used them to add up tax payments, engineers used them to calculate the amount of gravel they needed to build roads, and **merchants** used them to add up the bushels of grain they bought and sold.

Communicating before Computers

As more people learned how to read and write, written communication became increasingly common. Messages were recorded on clay tablets, **papyrus**, parchment, which was made from animal skins, and paper. Urgent warnings were sometimes sent by lighting signal fires on hilltops. These fires could be seen from miles away.

Rapid Communication

In 1844, a device known as the telegraph was perfected by American inventor Samuel Morse. The telegraph used electricity to send information rapidly over wires. Telegraph operators tapped out messages on a device called a telegraph key. They used a code of short and long signals, known as Morse code, to represent each letter of the alphabet. Far away at the receiving end, operators listened to the signals and wrote down the letters, or used automatic recording machines for the job.

In the 1870s, the invention of the telephone made it possible for people to speak — not just send codes — over wires. Telephone service was expensive and, at first, only businesses, government offices, and the wealthy could afford it. By 1900, people could use a new invention known as radio, or wireless communication. Radio carries information over long distances on invisible **electromagnetic waves** called radio waves. Today, computers, cell phones, and other devices use radio waves to connect to one another wirelessly.

(above) Messengers traveled long distances with letters about important events, contracts between merchants, and agreements negotiated with enemies and allies.

(right) Samuel Morse demonstrated his telegraph for the first time in 1838.

Calculating Machines

I n the 1600s and 1700s, some mathematicians invented mechanical devices that helped them do basic calculations needed for their own research and for jobs such as keeping tax records. Unfortunately, early calculating machines were expensive and unreliable because the precise gears and other metal parts that they required were almost impossible to make at the time.

A Tool for Multiplying

In 1617, Scottish mathematician John Napier devised an inexpensive tool called Napier's Rods, or Napier's Bones, to help with multiplying. Nine sticks or cylinders made of wood, bone, or ivory were marked with the multiplication tables for each digit from one through nine. When arranged properly, they could be used to solve difficult multiplication problems.

The Calculating Clock

In 1623, German mathematician, **linguist**, mapmaker, and **astronomer** Wilhelm Schickard designed a machine to help with complicated astronomical calculations. He called this the Calculating Clock. It combined Napier's Rods with gears and dials to do basic arithmetic. Sadly, Schickard died in 1635, and his work was destroyed in a fire shortly after. Knowledge of the Calculating Clock was lost until Schickard's notes were rediscovered in the 1950s.

Napier's Rods were popular during the 1600s with anyone doing difficult arithmetic, including students, astronomers, and bankers.

1685	1801	1890	1902	1906	1944	1947
Gottfried Leibniz designs his Stepped Reckoner, a mechanical calculator.	Joseph-Marie Jacquard automates weaving with a loom controlled by punch cards.	Herman Hollerith invents a punch-card system to analyze data.	Radio makes wireless communication possible.	Lee De Forest perfects the vacuum tube.	Construction begins on ENIAC, the first programmable electronic computer.	Researchers at Bell Laboratories invent the transistor.

The Pascaline

At age 19, French mathematician Blaise Pascal began to design a calculating machine, known as the Pascaline, to help his father with the endless sums required by his job as a tax collector. The Pascaline used **axles** and crown-shaped gears to add. A series of ratchets, which are small bars that catch the teeth of gears, carried numbers to the next column. With some extra steps, the Pascaline could be used to subtract as well.

Leibniz's Stepped Reckoner

Famous German mathematician Gottfried Leibniz felt that great minds were wasted doing hours of basic calculations, which he believed a machine could do just as well. In the 1680s, he experimented with several devices meant to do arithmetic. It is not certain if his best-known machine, the Stepped Reckoner, ever worked perfectly, but it was full of ideas that inspired other inventors.

(above) The Pascaline was too unreliable to become widely used, but Pascal's fame as a mathematician made scientists and mathematicians eager to study the Pascaline's design.

(below) Gottfried Leibniz's Stepped Reckoner used a complex system of gears in unusual shapes to add, subtract, divide, and multiply.

1957	1969	1974	1977	1983	1991	2000s
The integrated circuit begins a revolution in computer design.	The ARPANET becomes the first computer network.	Intel's 8080 processor chip begins the microcomputer age.	The Apple II becomes one of the first successful personal computers.	Two hundred computers connect to form the Internet.	Tim Berners-Lee begins the World Wide Web.	Memory chips become less expensive and more powerful.

Early Automation

The period from about 1750 to 1850 is known as the Industrial Revolution. During this time, the invention of machines powered by steam and water brought about great changes in the way things were made and the work people did.

Joseph-Marie Jacquard

Many new machines of the 1700s and 1800s were developed for the very important cloth industry. In 1801, a French weaver named Joseph-Marie Jacquard invented a **loom** that changed the way cloth was made. The loom was controlled by chains of stiff paper cards with small holes punched in them, now called punch cards or punched cards. The Jacquard loom made it possible to weave very complicated designs quickly and less expensively. A pattern was woven when the loom raised or lowered threads automatically according to patterns of holes punched into the cards.

Charles Babbage

In the 1600s and 1700s, **navigators**, engineers, and many others relied on books of mathematical tables to help them with their work. Often, people made mistakes when performing the calculations for the tables, copying the results by hand, and setting the numbers in metal **type** for printing. These mistakes caused shipwrecks and other misfortunes.

One skilled weaver was able to do the work of two using a Jacquard loom, so many workers lost their jobs.

Around 1820, a young English mathematician named Charles Babbage began planning a steam-powered machine, full of levers and gears, that would perform the calculations and press the answers directly onto metal plates, ready to be printed. Babbage tinkered with this machine, called the Difference Engine, for 20 years, but never completed it.

The Analytical Engine

By 1842, Babbage was planning an entirely new machine, the Analytical Engine. Unlike the Difference Engine, it was meant to be a programmable machine that could do almost any calculation. Its number memory, or store, was to hold 100 numbers up to 48 digits long. Sets of instructions, or programs, on punch cards controlled the mathematical operations. These operations took place in a part of the Engine dedicated to calculating, called the mill. The programs followed "recipes" for calculating, known as algorithms, as computer programs do today.

Charles Babbage spent a lifetime working on the Analytical Engine, which was still in pieces at the time of his death in 1871.

After each punch card was read and counted using Herman Hollerith's tabulator, an operator filed it in a sorting box for future use.

Herman Hollerith

Punch cards were not only used to control machines, but also to enter data, or information, into machines. Machines could then process, or analyze, the data automatically. American Herman Hollerith invented a punch card system for the United States Census Bureau, to tally and analyze **census** information collected in 1890. Punch cards containing data, such as the age, birthplace, and sex of citizens, were passed quickly through an electrical card-reader. Information on the cards was read by a tabulator, or counting device. Until the 1970s, any business collecting and analyzing large amounts of information, such as insurance companies and banks, used a punch card system based on Hollerith's.

The Computer Age

During World War II, governments gathered together their best mathematicians and engineers to design machines that would help them win the war. These included calculators powered by electricity, instead of metal gears or other mechanical parts, and the first digital computers.

Colossus

Mathematicians and engineers at a top-secret research center in England, called Bletchley Park, worked to break German and Japanese military codes in order to keep track of enemy ships and aircraft. They built a lightning-fast machine called the Colossus to look for patterns in coded messages. Cryptographers, or code breakers, used the patterns to help them crack codes much more quickly. Colossus had many computer-like features, including vacuum tube switches to control the flow of electricity and punched paper tape which, like punch cards, was used to enter data.

Alan Turing

Alan Turing was an English mathematician who, in 1936, showed that it was possible to solve almost all mathematical problems with a series of small steps in logic. This concept, now known as the Turing Machine, became an essential idea in computing. Turing later became part of the code-breaking team at Bletchley Park.

The Colossus contained about 2,000 vacuum tubes connected by wires and plugs.

ENIAC

At the same time that mathematicians and engineers were at work at Bletchley Park, groups of scientists funded by the Ballistics Research Laboratory (BRL), in the United States, were building many speedy new devices to produce the mathematical tables needed for ballistics, or the science of aiming weapons accurately. From 1943 to 1944, a BRL team at the University of Pennsylvania, led by engineers J. Presper Eckert and John Mauchly, designed a programmable, electronic device useful not only for ballistics but for many other types of calculations. This computer, called ENIAC, for Electronic Numerical Integrator and Computer, is usually considered the first electronic computer.

ENIAC used more than 18,000 vacuum tubes, weighed more than 30 tons (27 metric tons), and required enough electricity to power 30 homes. Technicians programmed it by plugging in electrical cables and flipping switches, which was a time-consuming job.

Although ENIAC seems very slow compared to a modern computer, it only required weeks to do calculations that would have taken mathematicians decades to do.

New Ideas

Even before ENIAC was completed, Eckert and Mauchly were planning a new machine, the Electronic Discrete Variable Automatic Computer (EDVAC). EDVAC's design had important new concepts that helped computers become faster and more reliable. For example, there was internal memory to store programs and data and a separate central processing unit (CPU), where calculations and other operations took place.

Early computers, such as the EDVAC, were hand-built using thousands of vacuum tubes and miles of wiring.

Computing Grows

Scientists who had worked on secret projects during World War II were filled with excitement about the newly invented electronic computer. They were eager to explore what computers could do not only during times of war, but during times of peace.

Moving On

Many scientists returned to universities and research centers, where they tested new ideas and built experimental computers that were faster, more reliable, and easier to program than wartime computers. Other inventors set up companies to design computers to sell to businesses and governments. Many companies that manufactured mechanical calculators and other business machines also entered the computing field, including International Business Machines (IBM). IBM soon became a major force in the computer industry.

UNIVAC

The inventors of ENIAC, J. Presper Eckert and John Mauchly, formed a company to build a new computer they called the UNIVAC (UNIVersal Automatic Computer). The UNIVAC I was designed to do everything from perform scientific calculations to print order forms, and was meant to be sold to businesses as well as to organizations conducting scientific research. Its central processing unit was about the size of a van and contained 5,200 vacuum tubes.

English mathematician Max Newman, who co-invented the Colossus, helped build the Manchester Mark I computer in the late 1940s. Eight were sold for atomic weapons research and other projects that required very complicated mathematical calculations.

An operator sitting at a central console controlled the UNIVAC I.

Room-sized Computers

Computers in the 1950s and 1960s were room-sized systems made up of many parts. These large machines were known as mainframes. Mainframes were kept in air-conditioned rooms so that they did not overheat, and were controlled by operators at consoles. The computers ran day and night, since restarting them, a process that involved flipping thousands of switches or plugging in cables, was very time-consuming.

The control panels of many early mainframes, such as this IBM 701, were covered with blinking lights, switches, and knobs.

Binary

Each computer understands only a code made up of 0s and 1s. The 0s and 1s are known as binary digits, or "bits" for short, and the code is called binary code. The 0s and 1s represent changes in the electric current that flows through the computer's circuits. Gates, or switches, control the flow of current in these circuits. When current passes through a gate, the switch is "on," which is represented by a 1. Electricity that is stopped is "off," which is represented by a 0.

Bits are organized into groups, or bytes, that are eight bits long. Within a computer, every number, letter, or symbol is represented by a byte or group of bytes. In addition, every action the computer is programmed to take is broken down into tiny steps, which are also represented by bytes.

Numeral	Binary Code
0	00110000
1	00110001
2	00110010
3	00110011
4	00110100
5	00110101
6	00110110
7	00110111
8	00111000
9	00111001

Programs and Data

At the beginning of the computer age, there was no such job as a "computer programmer," and no books or classes to teach programming skills. Through trial and error, early computer scientists learned to write programs that allowed computers to do very complex tasks. They also developed ways to store programs, as well as data, so that computers could access them quickly.

Early Programming Languages

At first, computer programs were written using machine language, the binary code of 0s and 1s. Writing a program with thousands of lines of 0s and 1s was very slow and confusing. Programmers soon developed many versions of a language called assembly language, which combines letters and numbers into easy-to-remember codes that represent each instruction. A program called an assembler translates the letter and number codes into binary code so that computers can understand them.

In the early 1950s, programmers began creating computer languages that used human words, phrases, and equations. These languages are known as higher-level languages. In 1964, John Kemeny and Thomas Kurtz, educators and mathematicians at Dartmouth College, in New Hampshire, invented the BASIC programming language. BASIC was the first higher-level programming language designed to be easy to learn and use. Today's higher-level languages include BASIC, Pascal, C, and Java.

Bugs

Grace Murray Hopper was a computer specialist who worked for the U.S. Navy. She was among the first to incorporate human language into computer programs. Hopper is also remembered for giving the name "bug" to a computer program error. One day in 1945, after setting 17,000 relays to program the Harvard Mark II, Hopper's work was ruined when a moth flew into the computer and caused a short circuit. Hopper's report, shown here with the moth, used the term "bug" to mean "an error in a computer program." "Bug" has the same meaning today.

Memory

The main, or internal, memory of the computer is where the computer holds programs and data that it is currently using. It is also where calculations are kept until they are needed to complete the job being processed.

For a computer to be fast, it must be able to reach anything in main memory almost instantly. For that reason, all main memory is designed to be Random Access Memory (RAM), which means that all the information in it can be reached directly. Most forms of RAM "forget," or are wiped clean, when the computer's power is turned off.

For more than 20 years, the most popular form of main memory was magnetic core memory. Core memory is RAM made of tiny metallic rings strung onto fine copper wires.

External storage, such as this hard disk from the 1970s, holds much more information than RAM and "remembers" even if the power is turned off, but it is much slower for the computer to access.

External Storage

A computer needs a device that can hold programs and data while they are not needed, so that they do not take up RAM and slow down processing times. Devices such as these are often called "external storage," because they are not part of the main computer. Many different types of external storage have been developed by computer manufacturers. The most important is the hard disk, which was invented in the 1950s by IBM. Disk drives began as fragile platters that measured nearly one yard (one meter) across, but they can now be small enough to fit in a pocket.

Transistors and Chips

The more circuits a computer has, the more information it can process and the faster it can process it. Early computers did not have room for many circuits because their thousands of vacuum tubes and miles of complicated wiring took up a lot of space. To make computers faster and more useful, a technical breakthrough was needed.

Transistors

In 1947, scientists at Bell Laboratories in New Jersey, the research division of the Bell Telephone Company, developed the transistor to replace the vacuum tube. Transistors are smaller than vacuum tubes, less expensive, and have no moving parts that wear out. They are made of **electrodes** attached to tiny layers of silicon or another **semi-conductor**. Computers with transistors became available in the late 1950s. They had far more circuits than computers with vacuum tubes, so they could process information much faster. They were also much smaller and less expensive than computers with vacuum tubes, so more businesses could afford them.

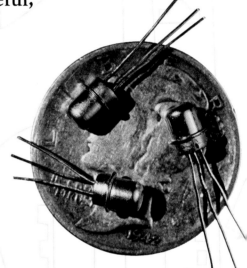

These transistors are so small that three can easily fit on a dime.

Early integrated circuits, such as this prototype of Jack Kilby's, held only a few transistors. Today's ICs may contain up to a billion transistors as well as other components.

Integrated Circuits

Computer manufacturers still faced a challenge. To make electrical circuits, workers had to connect thousands of transistors, by hand, to wires and other electrical components. The more wiring the electric current had to pass through, the slower the computer was. Around 1957, Robert Noyce of Fairchild Semiconductor and Jack Kilby of Texas Instruments each came up with a similar solution to the problem. They formed complete electrical circuits by embedding tiny transistors and other electrical components within tiny wafers of silicon. These are called integrated circuits (ICs), silicon chips, or microchips.

Memory Chips

Robert Noyce and others believed that integrated circuits could also be designed to do jobs that transistors could not do. Noyce formed his own company, Intel (for Integrated Electronics), to pursue that idea. In 1968, Intel marketed the first chip that was used as the computer's memory. By late 1970, a tiny RAM chip that could store 1,024 bits was available. Today, all RAM is located on chips.

In 1970, Intel invented another type of internal memory chip, the Read-Only Memory (ROM) chip. ROM chips hold the information that computers need to remember so that they can restart after they are turned off. With them, operators no longer had to restart computers by flipping switches or plugging in wire connectors.

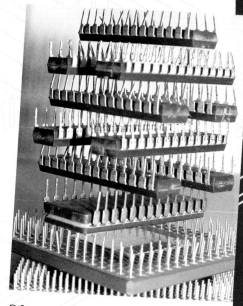

Silicon chips can be designed for different jobs, including logic operations, memory, and processing.

Microprocessor Chips

In the late 1960s, researchers speculated that a single chip could become an entire CPU, making it possible to build computers small enough to put into other devices. The first processor chip, the Intel 4004, became available in 1971. It had 2,300 transistors and could run small items such as hand-held calculators. Intel and a handful of other chip manufacturers improved processor chips until, in 1974, the first chips were released that were powerful enough to be used as a computer's CPU.

This worker is preparing the circular disks of silicon, called wafers, from which tiny silicon chips will be cut.

Computers for All

The silicon chip made it possible to build microcomputers, which are computers small enough to sit on a desk. More people began to use computers, and they discovered that, with a computer's help, they could do difficult jobs far more quickly than they could on their own.

The Microcomputer Arrives

Electronics hobbyists and scientists were eager to experiment and play with computers at home. Around 1974, some small companies began to sell basic home computers that used processor chips such as the Intel 8080. A few fully assembled home computers were available, but most were build-it-yourself kits that people purchased from electronics hobby stores or by mail. Owners of early home computers wrote their own programs, usually in assembly language. Writing programs was difficult, so people found it challenging to get their computers to do something as simple as add or print out a series of numbers.

HOW TO "READ" FM TUNER SPECIFICATIONS

Popular Electronics

WORLD'S LARGEST-SELLING ELECTRONICS MAGAZINE   JANUARY 1975/75¢

PROJECT BREAKTHROUGH!

World's First Minicomputer Kit to Rival Commercial Models...

"ALTAIR 8800"   SAVE OVER $1000

ALTAIR 8800

ALSO IN THIS ISSUE:
- An Under-$90 Scientific Calculator Project
- CCD's—TV Camera Tube Successor?
- Thyristor-Controlled Photoflashers

TEST REPORTS:
Technics 200 Speaker System
Pioneer RT-1011 Open-Reel Recorder
Tram Diamond-40 CB AM T...
Edmund Scientifi...
Hewlett-Packard...

The Boom Begins

In 1976, Steve Jobs and Stephen Wozniak formed Apple Computers, a two-man company based in the Jobs' family garage. Their goal was to build microcomputers that everyone could use, not just experts and hobbyists. Their first computer was the basic Apple I. Next, they built the Apple II. Unlike the Apple I, the Apple II came completely preassembled, with easy-to-use software already installed. When the Apple II was connected to a color TV screen, it could display images in color, which was rare for any computer at the time. Many artists, teachers, and writers bought the Apple II as their first computer.

One of the earliest and most popular kit computers was the Altair 8800. It was first sold in 1975 for less than $500.

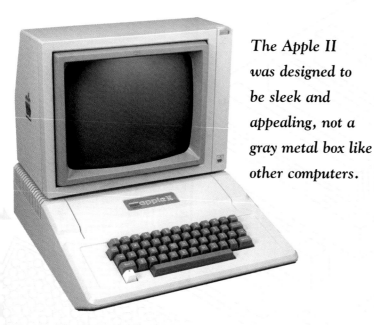

The Apple II was designed to be sleek and appealing, not a gray metal box like other computers.

The IBM PC

By the early 1980s, large companies that built mainframes were designing microcomputers. In 1981, computing giant IBM released its personal computer, the IBM PC. The PC could be used by people at home and in small businesses to perform many different tasks, including keeping accounts and inventories and writing letters.

After its release, more than 1.5 billion IBM PCs and PC copies, known as clones, were sold in office supply stores and department stores.

Douglas Engelbart

Douglas Engelbart was an American researcher who made many important contributions to the development of computers. In the 1960s, he invented on-screen windows. Windows are framed work areas that can appear on the screen at the same time. Users can move from one window to another to switch between tasks.

In the 1970s, Engelbart's ideas inspired researchers at Xerox to develop the first graphical user interface, or GUI (pronounced "goo'-ee"). A GUI is a way of communicating with a computer using images, such as icons, or pull-down menus of commands. Non-experts find it easier to use a GUI than to type in complicated commands.

Douglas Engelbart also invented the computer mouse, which people use to move from one window to another.

Inside a Computer

People use personal computers every day at work, in school, and at home. In this model from the early 2000s, the actual computer, including the CPU and memory, is inside a protective case. The monitor, keyboard, printer, and mouse are connected to the computer with cables. They are used to input and output data and programs.

1. Motherboard: Since the 1970s, computers have been made by attaching silicon chips, or integrated circuits, to circuit boards. The main circuit board, called the motherboard, contains the central processor (CPU) and memory chips for RAM and ROM.

2. CD-ROM drive: The CD-ROM drive reads information stored on CDs and is often used to install new programs.

Inkjet printer: An inkjet printer (not shown) shoots tiny amounts of ink onto paper to produce color and black-and-white documents. It was invented in the late 1970s by computer company Hewlett-Packard, but it took more than ten years of further development before it was ready to be sold to the public.

3. The hard drive: The computer's hard drive stores large amounts of data magnetically. The disk spins extremely fast when it is in use, so it is sealed in a metal container to prevent it from spinning out of the computer and to protect its sensitive magnetic surface from dust.

4. The keyboard: Computer keyboards evolved from the keyboards of typewriters, which were developed in the late 1860s by American inventor Christopher Sholes. Keyboards are used to type information into computers. Their keys can be programmed to represent even more numbers, letters, and symbols than those shown.

5. Mouse: The movement of the mouse controls the position of the cursor on the screen. Clicking the mouse's buttons gives commands to the computer.

6. Monitor: This computer monitor is made up of a cathode ray tube (CRT), which is the same technology as that used in many televisions. The CRT uses an electron gun in a vacuum tube to create images on the screen. The images are made up of glowing dots called pixels.

Computer Software

A computer is just a box full of electronic components, known as hardware, until someone programs it with software that tells it what to do and how to do it. A program can be as short as a few lines or longer than a dictionary.

Operating Systems

The operating system (OS) is the software that organizes the way a computer receives and stores information, how it uses its internal memory, and how it interacts with the hard drive, keyboard, and other pieces of equipment. The OS also controls all the other programs on the computer. If the operating system is not working properly, the computer will be difficult to use, or not work at all. Common operating systems include Microsoft Windows, Linux, and Apple's Mac OS.

In 1991, Linus Torvalds, a student at the University of Finland, released Linux, an operating system inspired by the popular Unix OS.

Applications Software

Once an operating system is running, programs known as application, can be installed to do many kinds of tasks. People write and edit stories, letters, and reports using word-processing applications. Multimedia applications make it possible to draw, change photographs, edit and store music, and watch DVDs. Engineers and architects use computer-assisted design (CAD) programs to produce detailed three-dimensional images, which software can turn into plans for buildings, airplanes, and household products.

Designers and commercial artists use applications software when preparing advertisements, magazines, posters, and books.

A Software Empire

While in high school in Seattle, Bill Gates and his classmate Paul Allen came up with the idea of building a business based on computer programming. Gates left Seattle to attend Harvard University in 1973, but he continued to focus on his computer projects with Allen. Within a year, he and Allen had been hired to write BASIC for the Altair 8800 microcomputer. Gates left Harvard and, in 1975, formed Microsoft Corporation in Seattle with Allen. Today, Microsoft is one of the world's wealthiest corporations.

Bill Gates, shown here, Paul Allen, and businessman Steve Ballmer built Microsoft into the world's largest software corporation.

Computer Games

Almost as soon as computers were invented, programmers began writing games to play on them. Today, games are among the most popular applications. Early games had no drawings, just very simple graphics made from the characters on a computer keyboard. Today's computer games, which are written by teams of game designers, artists, and programmers, have detailed, full-color graphics and realistic-looking motion.

Viruses and Worms

Viruses and worms are programs that copy themselves and spread wherever there is contact with another computer. They can be used to steal private information, damage files, or make computer networks so busy that people cannot connect to them.

Many types of computer games are available, including card games and simulation games.

Viruses and worms are written by people known as hackers. Early computer hackers were programmers playing with computer codes and having fun learning what computers could do. Today, the term "hacking" often refers to behavior that is deliberately harmful and is sometimes considered a crime.

A Connected World

Computer networks make it possible to communicate with friends, learn news, and do business with people from all over the globe. To make networking possible, computer scientists had to invent ways for computers to communicate with one another.

The First Computer Network

The first computer network, called the ARPANET (Advanced Research Projects Agency NETwork), was established in 1969 by the U.S. Department of Defense. The Department wanted to be able to quickly move military information from one location to another in case of a war or natural disaster. The ARPANET connected four computers at universities working on projects for the Department of Defense. Researchers working on the projects discovered that it was convenient to use the ARPANET to send information and messages, and they encouraged others to try it.

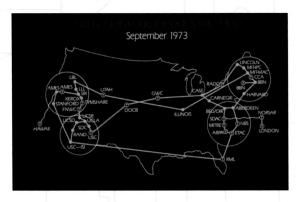

September 1973

The ARPANET slowly expanded to include other universities and laboratories, as shown in this map. Eventually, other networks were formed as well.

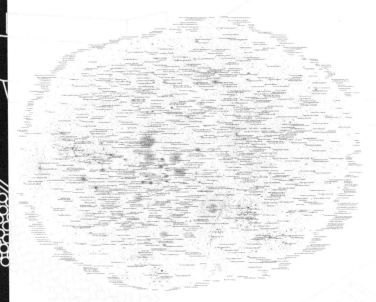

This map of the world's Internet traffic shows the complex spiderweb of connections that make it possible to link distant computers.

The Internet

In 1983, several networks with a total of 200 computers decided to join together and form an international network called the Internet. Today, more than one billion people use the Internet through computers at home, school, libraries, and work. The most popular use for the Internet is sending and receiving e-mail. The speed of the Internet also makes it possible for people on opposite sides of the world to play computer games together or to "chat," or have an online typed conversation in real time.

The World Wide Web

The Internet is one of the easiest ways to gather information from around the world. The information, which includes documents on hundreds of thousands of topics, electronic books, music and video files, newspapers, and much more, is part of the World Wide Web. The World Wide Web, or Web for short, was invented in 1989 by an English computer scientist named Tim Berners-Lee. Berners-Lee promoted the idea of people sharing knowledge through a "web" of documents, to be stored on computers called servers throughout the Internet.

Berners-Lee also invented Hypertext Mark-up Language (HTML) as a tool to prepare Web pages, or online documents. A Web page contains codes that turn words or images into "hypertext," which are links that take the reader to text, pictures, music, and video files elsewhere in the document, or even other places on the Web. Before HTML, documents on computers were read the same way as books: one page after another, one document at a time. In addition, Berners-Lee and his colleagues devised a system that gave each Web page its own address, called a Uniform Resource Locator (URL), and wrote the first browser, a type of applications software needed to read Web documents stored at servers.

Tim Berners-Lee invented the World Wide Web while working at CERN, the European Organization for Nuclear Research, in Switzerland.

Search Engines

The Web is such a vast sea of information that, without help, people would never find the information they need. Search engines, such as Google and Yahoo, are programs that provide that help. They use complicated formulas to find documents or websites that match key words users enter into the search engine.

Instant messaging allows people to send and receive text over the Internet in real time. People can chat with friends, or with members of groups that share their interests.

At Work and Play

From early prototypes to the portable versions we use today, computers have changed the way we work and play. Not only do they make some jobs faster and easier, but they make entirely new kinds of jobs possible. Researchers in universities and the computer industry continue to explore new uses for computers.

Computers for Banking

In the 1970s, machines called ATMs (Automated Teller Machines) or ABMs (Automated Banking Machines) began to change the way people banked. People no longer had to go to their banks and wait for tellers to serve them. Using ATMs, which have computers inside that do many of the same jobs as tellers, people could deposit checks, withdraw money, or pay bills on their own at any time of day or night.

Since online banking arrived in the late 1990s, customers have been able to pay their bills and transfer money from one account to another over the Internet. The Internet also links stores with banks, making it possible for shoppers to purchase items by transferring money from their bank accounts to the stores' bank accounts, using a debit card.

(right) With VR, special helmets or visors show images that give people playing computer games the feeling of moving through realistic three-dimensional space.

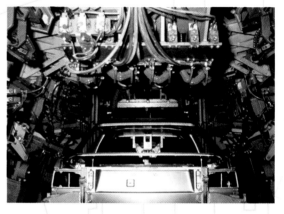

(above) Computerized robotic arms, such as these in an automobile factory, do dangerous or repetitive jobs on assembly lines that people used to do.

Virtual Reality Simulations

Virtual Reality (VR) simulations use computer hardware and software to create sights, sounds, and sometimes movements that seem real. Many VR simulations are used to train people for risky jobs. Pilots learn to fly airplanes using simulators, and surgeons practice difficult procedures using VR, before operating on real patients. VR simulations also help engineers test equipment that will be used in outer space or deep underwater.

Computers and the Arts

For hundreds of years, people composing music wrote out each note by hand, which was a very time-consuming process. Today, composers use special software to help them write down the notes of songs and arrange the music. Computers play back the arranged pieces so that composers can hear how they sound. Artists also use computers to create their work. Using a stylus, which looks like a pen, they draw pictures on special tablets connected to their computers. The drawings are saved in the computers, and graphics software is used to color them. Computers are also used to edit photographs, for example to lighten photos that are too dark or to make blurry images appear sharper.

(right) Using computers, artists can create images that include patterns, called fractals, which are based on mathematical formulas.

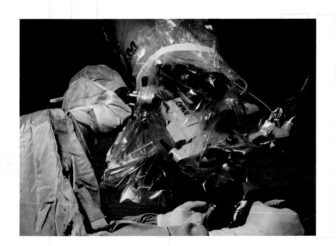

(above) Surgeons doing delicate brain surgery sometimes use joystick controllers connected to robotic microsurgery equipment.

Computers for Medicine

Computers are used to help doctors perform surgery that is too delicate for human hands to manage, such as repairing tiny blood vessels. This surgery, called microsurgery, is controlled by a human surgeon looking through a microscope. Computer software converts the surgeon's motions into tiny movements of a computer-controlled robotic arm. Surgeons also use robotic arms to perform medical procedures on patients in other locations. The first remote robotic surgery took place in 1997, when a surgeon in Italy operated on a patient 620 miles (1,000 kilometers) away.

Invisible Computers

Many computers are completely invisible to us. Inventors have found ways to incorporate tiny microprocessors inside everyday items, from cell phones to cars, to make new features possible.

In Transportation

Automobile manufacturers began to place microprocessors in cars around 1980, using them to regulate a car engine's fuel mix. This helped improve gas mileage and reduce **emissions** that cause air pollution. Today, the average car contains more than 40 microprocessors, which control radios and automatic door locks, decide if air bags should inflate, check if a car's anti-locking braking systems (ABS) should activate to reduce the chance of skidding, and much more.

In most large aircraft, computers, microprocessors, and sensors have replaced many of the levers, cables, and mechanical controls that pilots once used to control the plane's moving parts. In some planes, onboard computers actually do most of the flying, including takeoffs and landings.

(above) A tiny microprocessor and memory chip make it possible to use a cell phone as an address book, a calculator, and even a camera.

(left) Airplanes have multiple computers and wires for every part of the system in case something fails.

Data on a Card

"Smart cards" are plastic cards that look like credit cards. Inventors in several countries began to design these cards, which contain memory chips, microprocessors, and powerful security software, in the early 1970s. In France, in the 1980s, smart cards were promoted as a way to pay for bus trips, movies, and groceries. Today, they are becoming more widely used as a way to transport money and private information digitally. For example, smart cards can hold a person's complete medical history, so that it is available whenever a doctor needs it.

(right) Microprocessors in tiny portable music players make it possible to organize favorite songs into playlists, and search for specific songs.

Just for Fun

Many electronic entertainment devices and toys contain microprocessors. Portable music players with microprocessors store and play music. Some music players are powerful enough to show videos as well. Microprocessor-based DVD players and digital video recorders (DVRs) allow users to watch movies or favorite TV shows whenever they want. Microprocessors in talking and moving toys enable them to say programmed words and phrases, respond to voice commands, and receive commands from wireless remote controls.

(above) This toy is controlled by a tiny half-inch by half-inch (14-millimeter by 14-millimeter) microprocessor that helps it recognize human speech so that it can respond to spoken commands.

New Uses for Microprocessors

Inventors are constantly experimenting with new ways to incorporate microprocessors in tools and gadgets. A hand-held telescope will soon be available that makes stargazing interactive. Focus the telescope on a star and the telescope provides information about the star in computer-generated speech and displays star maps as well as other information. Inventors are also working on a toothbrush that is programmed to recognize correct brushing and reward users with a song.

In the Future

Inventors are always exploring new ideas in computing. Some work alone, while others work with teams of scientists, engineers, and designers at major computer companies. Each year, these companies present their new products and ideas for future products at exhibitions and conventions.

Computers on the Go

At home or away, people want their computers nearby. Computers are getting sleeker and small enough to be carried in backpacks or even pockets. Today's lightweight laptops or notebook computers have flat, **liquid crystal display** (LCD) screens that are no thicker than a magazine, instead of bulky CRT screens.

Today's portable computers have more computing power than mainframes had 20 years ago.

Staying Connected

Less than 15 years ago, most computers were not connected to other computers. Today, many inventors are developing tiny, portable devices so that people can send e-mail, watch online TV, chat, and listen to music wherever there is a wireless Internet connection. Wireless technology also makes new services possible, such as broadcasting weather warnings and traffic reports to onboard car computers. Researchers even hope to make highways safer by automating them. Instead of cars being controlled by drivers, they would be controlled by a central computer that is connected wirelessly to the vehicles.

Researcher Ruth Kikin-Gil invented "Buddy Beads" so that friends could communicate with one another using wireless technology. When one friend presses on beads on his or her bracelet, beads on the other friend's bracelet light up and send a coded message.

RFID Chips

In the 1970s, two American inventors developed Radio-Frequency IDentification (RFID) chips, based on technology developed during World War II. These chips transmit identification information using radio waves. Some grocery packages have RFID chips, with the grocery item's product number, inside. This way, businesses can know when the packages are taken out of the store, and restock. RFID chips can also be implanted in people, so that their identities and locations can be monitored. Many people are concerned about RFID because they feel that the technology will cause a loss of privacy and freedom.

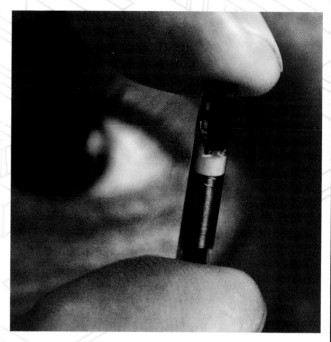

(above) Radio-frequency Identification chips, such as these, can be placed inside a capsule and safely inserted under the skin. RFID implants are already used to tag cats and dogs with their owners' names and addresses, so that animal shelters and veterinarians can reunite lost pets with their owners.

The Next Revolution

Computers will become even smaller with the growth of nanotechnology, the science of building objects with materials that are no larger than molecules and atoms. Engineers, chemists, biologists, and other types of scientists have been working together in this new field since American scientist K. Eric Drexler first suggested nanotechnology in 1981. Nanoscale materials are already used in the semiconductors of the smallest chips.

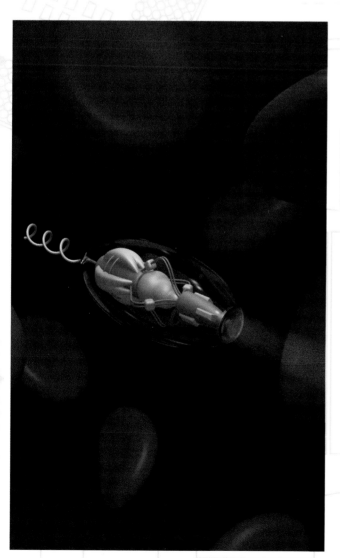

(left) Scientists expect that doctors will one day be able to inject thousands of nanocomputers into the human body, to identify cancer cells and destroy them one by one.

Glossary

astronomer A person who studies the stars, planets, and moons

axle A pole or bar on which a wheel turns

census An official survey or count of a population done by a government

circuit The complete route that an electric current travels

console A panel with switches and dials for controlling an electronic or mechanical device

digital Relating to the processing, storing, or transmitting of data in the form of numerical digits

electrode A solid connector, such as a metal wire, which conducts electricity in and out of devices such as transistors

electromagnetic wave A wave of energy made up of electric and magnetic fields

emissions Fumes and gases released into the air

engineer A person who designs or creates buildings, machines, and other manufactured items

Incan Of or related to the Inca, a native people of Peru whose empire lasted until the mid-1500s

linguist A person who studies human speech

liquid crystal display (LCD) A display on an electronic device consisting of liquid crystal. The display darkens in areas where an electric current passes through the liquid crystal, and an image is created by the combination of light and dark areas

logic A system of reasoning based on sets of rules

loom A device used to weave thread or yarn into cloth

mechanical Operated by machinery

merchant A person who buys and sells goods

navigator A person trained in navigation, the science of directing ships, aircraft, or other vehicles from one place to another

papyrus A writing material made from the papyrus plant, a tall plant that grows along the Nile River, in Egypt

relay A mechanical switch that can be set to "on" or "off" to control the flow of electric current

semiconductor A material through which electricity flows, though more slowly than through conductors

type A block, usually made from metal, with a raised letter or number that is inked and used to print

World War II A war fought by countries around the world from 1939 to 1945

Index

Printed in the U.S.A.

Zutphen District